Soul Deep

Poetry

By Connie Howell

DEEP READ PRESS
LAFAYETTE, TENNESSEE
deepreadpress@gmail.com

The Publisher offers discounts for bulk orders.

First Deep Read Press Edition

Manufactured in the United States of America

Deep Read Press

www.deepreadpress.com

615-670-1725

ISBN: 978-1-954989-27-6

Cover Design by: Kim Gammon

Cover Image by: Connie Laswell

Published by:

DEEP READ PRESS

Lafayette, Tennessee

www.deepreadpress.com

deepreadpress@gmail.com

For: Poetry lovers wherever you are, may the love of verse connect us in Spirit.

Choices

I choose love over fear,
To cherish those I hold dear,
Peace instead of war,
Hope rather than despair,
Having a care
For each other.

I want joy and happiness,
A hand to hold and caress,
So, let me be clear,
I choose love over fear,
Every time.

Sleep Peacefully

Sleep peacefully my beloved,
Go on to joys unknown,
Awake and find your dream come true
Of loved ones all around,
And when you have a moment
A thought to each of us,
To bring us close re-union
From time to time.

Sleep peacefully my beloved,
And walk amongst the flowers,
Of hue beyond description
And smell beyond compare,
And when you have a moment
A thought to each of us,
To bring us close re-union
From time to time.

Sleep peacefully my beloved,
And as you go away,
Look back with joy not sorrow,
Of times of different sway,
And when you have a moment
A thought to each of us,
To bring us close re-union
From time to time.

Grief

My soul is open,
My emotions are bare,
My heart's full of sadness
Yet I know that it's fair,
I don't blame anyone,
For I know the time's come,
My mother must leave us
And go on elsewhere,
My sadness will go,
And love will abide,
To bring my dear mother
Again, by my side,
I will thank then my spirit,
For its wisdom and care,
To bring hope out of sorrow
And love from despair.

Helpless

I looked upon his worried brow,
And wished that I could help,
For I could feel within my soul,
The need for calming words.
I hadn't seen him care so much
For so many years,
And yet I knew I couldn't say
The words he had to hear,
For only he could speak the sound
With inspirational aid,
I knew I had to stand aside,
Until the worry passed.

Love Comes Again

Another promise made not kept,
Time, and time again, I wept,
At disappointments come and gone
Wanting apology
But there was none.

I cried the tears of sorrows pain,
My heart felt like it was mortally slain,
And doubting that I would ever know,
The love I craved and wanted so.

But life went on though I wished it not,
And broken, wounded, scarred a lot,
Love came once more with someone new,
Then finally without pain, I remembered you.

Thankful that I had escaped your cruel grasp,
A softer hand and heart to clasp
Was given to me, as if a prize,
For surviving and transcending all your lies.

Daisy Chain

Daisy chain necklace made lovingly with care,
I was a child who loved to dance with nature and its creatures,
Bluebell wood was understood to be a magic place,
And under leaves of ferns and plants,
Lived fairies in their splendour.

Pain

Pain, like tiny shards of glass,
Piercing every vein,
No mercy, no reprieve,
Just endless suffering.

Though I am not alone in feeling pain,
I have no comfort or companionship,
I am isolated in my world,
Of agony.

I see no one, I hear no one,
I am too distressed,
To see or hear anything,
Except my pain.

Uncertainty

Sometimes, it is hard to know what to do.
Which way to go, how to proceed.
Frightening times bring fear and uncertainty.
What are we to do, how do we act?
Life is full of uncertainty, yet we push against it,
Hoping to control every aspect of life,
Living peacefully, with feeling uncertain,
Is an art, yet to be perfected by me, and most of you.

Eeenie, Meenie, Miney Mo

Eeenie, Meenie, Miney Mo,
A little rhyme said long ago,
I was a child with childish ways,
So long ago, so many days,
Gone by.
Now I'm grown, but still a child,
A little mischief still inside,
A happy place for me to go,
With Eenie, Meenie, Miney Mo.

The Drinker

Whatever was he thinking,
Staying out till midnight drinking?
While his wife and children waited patiently,
They loved him none the less,
Though he caused them much distress
Because sober he was charm personified.
He was famous down the pub,
Which was his usual social hub,
Where no one could throw darts the way he did.

He often spent his money,
Leaving nothing for his honey
To buy shopping for the growing family
Though this may sound quite sad
And indeed, it's kind of bad,
It's a story told so often round the world,
Now I'm not into preaching,
Though by now you may be screeching,
Whatever was he thinking,
Staying out 'til midnight drinking.

I Must Go

Let me go, I cannot stay,
I must move forward,
My spirit calls me home.

I loved you once, I didn't know better,
But I need to be free, to be fully me.

It served me once to be with you,
But I struggled with confinement,
I need to stretch my wings and fly,
You will understand, as time goes by.

I Was Lost

I lost myself, so long ago,
I couldn't find the way back home.
I wandered lonely, I suffered long,
Before I found the road to walk.

Each day, each step brought me closer,
But the road was long and sometimes dark,
I travelled on by day and night,
At last, I knew the way.

The light was lit inside of me,
I was ready to give it all,
To reach inside and find again,
The me, I longed to be.

Parents

What are parents?
Two people joined together,
A vehicle in which to travel,

A chance to live,
A journey from the known
To the unknown.

Beauty

What is beauty?
A pretty face or something else.
Do you feel beauty, do you see beauty?
It's like love, everyone has a different interpretation.
Beauty can be a desire,
A need to find our inner selves,
Which are beautiful, each in their way.
Beaut-i-ful, full of vitality,
Serenity, peace and quiet.
Whatever your concept of beauty,
Keep it within yourself and cherish it,
For if you recognize beauty,
You recognize Godliness.

Two Little Kittens

Two little kittens playing on the deck,
One called Tiddles one called Speck,
Jumping and rolling, playing peek a boo
Meowing, chewing, on an old shoe.

The morning Sun shines brightly,
The kittens are still sprightly,
Playful and amusing making people smile,
Their energy levels still high for a while.

Then tiredness comes a calling
Their eyelids are now falling,
So, they settle down to sleep,
And their slumber is quite deep.

Two little kittens sleeping on the deck,
One called Tiddles one called Speck.

The Owl

The owl watches eagerly
Waiting for prey to show itself.
It is hidden to most eyes,
Only those that look hard could see,
The beautiful face and wings
Ready to fly in an instant.

Called the eagle of the night,
The owl watches for the tiniest movement
Then silently and swiftly it has its meal,
And then goes back to its vantage point,
Until the next unsuspecting creature
Catches the all-seeing eyes.

Insects

Insects crawling, hurrying scurrying,
This way that way, carrying food.
Big ones, little ones, funny shaped black ones
Withering, dithering, finding mates.
Ants and beetles, flies, and mosquitoes
Flying things with big fat wings,
Busy, busy, always busy,
Getting on with nature's way.
Eating, feeding, sometimes misleading,
Insects can be annoying things.
Exploring toes, and legs and dresses
Tickling, itching here and there,
Giving me moments of interest and mystery,
Wondering about their history
Back I go to watch some more,
Insect habitats on the floor.

Rainbow

Rain fell lightly, wetting me slightly,
Appearing majestically the sun dominated once again,
I looked in awe at seven heavenly colours,
Never-before had they seemed so vivid,
Before me was a miracle of nature
Of such beauty it made me gasp,
Wanting nothing more than it should last.

The Magpie

The Magpie sings his melodious song,
So sweet and yet so very strong
Then pauses long enough to hear,
If any other song is near.

I dig for weeds, he digs for food,
Side by side, in shared neighbourhood
Not too close but sharing space,
Is this mine, his, or our place.

In harmony we get along
He sings, I listen to his song,
It fills me with music that I lack,
It makes me want to get it back.

To share with you and everyone
To sing until my voice is gone,
Then you can listen and make your own
Sweet music that may be unknown.

For each of us has our own tune
I hope you let yours out soon,
A chorus we can together make,
And sing the songs with soulful story.

Wind Song

You blow so fiercely you howl so loudly,
The leaves are scurrying, no control,
I wonder where you come from and where you go,
And how you change from friend to foe.

What is your song, I can't quite get it,
What rhythm is it that you drum?
Should I be frightened or grateful that I'm inside?
Shall I peak or shall I hide?

You come you go the trees sway strongly,
Teaching me the way to bend
Flexibility at its best
Then you leave and we can rest.

The Little Flower

There was a little flower,
It was growing all alone
She couldn't find her family,
She thought they'd all left home,
The birds would come and sing to her,
With songs that were divine
And she came to know that family,
Was around her all the time.

Daisy Chain

Daisy chain necklace made lovingly with care,
I was a child who loved to dance with nature and its creatures,
Bluebell wood was understood to be a magic place,
And under leaves of ferns and plants,
Lived fairies in their splendour.

The Butterfly

Wings of delicate beauty,
Fluttering here and there,
Once you were a chrysalis,
Transforming in your cocoon.
No one on the outside,
Could see you as you changed.

Then out you came,
And spread your wings,
Then they were all amazed.
Transformed from one thing to another,
Your true self dressed in brilliant colour,
That is true alchemy.

The Lake

Gentle ripples flow along,
Lapping sounds and sacred song,
If I look with open eyes
I see reflected trees and sky,
With my eyes closed and calm
The soft rhythmic rippling is like a balm,
It nourishes mind and soul so deep,
And goes with me, mine to always keep.

The Train Ride

I was on the train today reading my book,
Three women got on with bags and cups,
They had each bought a coffee to drink,
But then had to juggle the bags and think,
How to do both at the same time.

I watched in amusement and was happy enough,
I gathered they could manage their stuff,
I read on while they settled themselves down.
They started to natter with much lively chatter,
Whilst sitting beneath the "quiet carriage" sign.

Hmm I thought to myself this doesn't seem quiet,
It resembles a little riot, they simply ignored the sign,
I decided to read on, but the words wouldn't gel,
So, I thought what the hell and
I put down my book, I gave them a look,
And I smiled.

The Fly

Oh, my said the fly as it sat upon the ceiling,
That human on the chair down there,
Is looking quite appealing,
Perhaps I'll buzz and flap my wings,
And let him know I'm friendly,
I know that humans don't like flies,
So, I'll land on him quite gently.

Oh, my said the human,
As he watched the fly come over,
He didn't quite know what to do,
So, he tried to duck for cover,
But the fly was quick and agile,
And landed on his nose,
And the human, watched in awe, then he
Momentarily froze.

So, eye to eye or nose to nose,
The two of them were silent,
The fly was calmly sitting,
and the human wasn't violent,
He was amazed as both they gazed,
Into each other's faces,
And both of them began to think,
What fun if they'd trade places.

Hats

Which of my hats will I wear today?
Am I feeling in the pink or red with delight?
Grey like the weather or black like the night.
So many roles these hats of mine play
Author, wife, mother, sister, and friend.

I look in the mirror and remember Peru,
The Andes Mountains are a stunning view,
My hats give me flashbacks of wonderful times,
They spark littles ditties and playful rhymes.
How many hats will you wear today?
One or two or give them all away.

How would it be with no hats to wear?
I'll ponder on it now while I put a hat on.
I remember a time when I had none,
Now a collection appears at my front door,
I wonder if I'll be tempted to buy any more.

I think I need purple, orange, or green,
Well, you know how it is when you want to be seen,
OMG, now I'm addicted to getting more hats,
Flamboyant and cheeky, demure, and outrageous.
I never knew I could be quite so courageous.

See you later I am off to the shops.

LOL

My sides are splitting, I am laughing so hard,
I just received the funniest card,
From my friend.

She knows me so well,
From the card I can tell
She really knows.

That I am quirky and silly,
And I am not composed,
Then, I have to go pee.

Legs crossed or a flood will occur,
And that would certainly cause a stir,
Then I would lol so much more.

The Collective Nightmare

I am bathed in sweat,
People are screaming, running for their lives,
The fear is palpable, contagious.

I try to find somewhere to hide,
But it is too late the enemy is already inside of me,
It goes wherever I go.

The adrenaline pumps rapidly through every cell
Terror makes me want to keep on moving,
To get away
Even though I can't see who or what it is, that
pursues us.

My own private hell rages until I finally say,
Enough, I cannot live this way a moment longer,
And I wake up, relieved to have escaped the torturous
depths to which I'd plunged.

I see the daylight streaming in and realise, that I have
been dreaming,
I give thanks that I am safe and that,
I don't have to go back there anymore.

A Silent Friend

Death came, it was a surprise,
Even though expected, it came like a thief in the night.
And my breath was taken away,
By the suddenness, the surety of it,
No hesitation, it was time, so it came and took its prize.

It made me think of mortality,
Mine, yours, ours.
How to prepare, if at all
Without losing the reality of life.
To look death in the face and to know
That when it comes it will not be a stranger,
But rather a friend who has waited patiently, silently,
For reunion.

Questions

Pen poised, mind alert,
What should I write of next?
The colours of the rainbow,
The wonders of the world.
The ups and downs of people,
Of animals and trees
We're all of one big universe,
One great and wondrous plan,
We interlock and interweave,
And play all different parts,
We question and we answer,
And try to find out things,
Quite often we misjudge them,
Sometimes we understand,
But mysteries will stay the same,
Until we see the plan.

To Those in Need

Come, let me touch you,
And heal your hurts,
Let me spread my wings around you,
Protecting you from life's sad days
And baffling ways,
I am a shelter,
Please come,
Abide within my loving arms,
Secured against my breast,
I'll love you and enfold you,
Until it's time to go
To meet again the challenges
With strength renewed once more,
And as you go along your way,
Look back from time to time,
And see me as your beacon,
Between this life and Divine
For I am in the middle
Of this world and the next,
And I can help you always,
By bridging rivers deep.

The Masters Voice

The master's voice is calling,
You hear it in your mind,
It doesn't matter who he is,
As long, as he is kind,
The words are meant to help you,
To inspire the courage great
And sweetness will surround you,
Until your hour of fate.

Heavenly Telephone

Ring, ring telephone
Call me up and tell me more,
Talk to me about life's dreams,
Let me know of my Souls theme,
I am listening as before,
Ever tuned to hearing more,
Thirsty for the knowledge of life
And death, and all the glorious beings
Let me hear some more.

Full Moon

Here you are again,
Shining so brightly keeping me awake,
And illuminating my mind
Thoughts running rampant through the night,
No rest just unbridled thinking.

Yet
You are so beautiful how can I be angry?
There you are in your house,
Lighting up our world in part
While your brother sun shines on the other side
Giving light of a different kind.

Either way none can hide from the glow
Though some may sleep, not me,
I am energized by your light,
I do not know why I can't let go,
So here we are, companions once more.

The Spectre

Spectre of the past
Haunting me
It seems quite daunting,
But once my fear is conquered
I see a friendly face,
In fears place
And I am strong.

The Thoughts

In the haze of a smoky past,
Thoughts come again, but they don't last,
I contemplate, then let them go,
For holding on just keeps me bound, And I am now
free of the merry go round.
Even though good thoughts come, I release them
wanting none,
So that I can remain in the here and now.

Kaleidoscope

A kaleidoscope of colour
reigning down upon my soul,
My arms are open wide,
so that my heart can make me whole,
Once more.
I lost myself a hundred times,
yet I stand before you now,
Again, you call my spirit, for you know just when and
how I need your warm embrace.
And you come.

The Shadow

In the shadow my music waits to be played,
When the time is right.
Will you like it? I don't know.
But I will compose it,
Even though I may not have an audience.
I will hear it in the night,
As it caresses my brain with starlight.
And the joy of creation is expressed,
From my soul.

The Song

The words will not come,
when I write it comes out wrong
How can I tell you what I really feel, what you mean to me,
If I could, I would harmonize my words in a song,
A melody so beautiful
You would swoon with delight,
And both our souls would unite and be free
Together.

Yearning

I yearn to know you, yet you are elusive.
How do I grasp what cannot be held?
How do I know the unknowable?
And yet,
I feel you, with my other senses,
You live within my heart,
You sing to me with soundless words,
And,
I almost understand,
That which has no understanding.

The Voice

What is this voice that calls me from my soul?
Sometimes my ears cannot discern the nature of it all,
I follow it because I know, it leads me not astray.
Thought sometimes it is frightening,
Not knowing where it leads,
I must go and be transformed by it,
And enjoy each precious day.

Red Chakra

Red light, shining bright,
Slow and steady wins the race,
Grounding roots, strong ties
Let me know I can survive.
Family ties, tribal dance
Dare I take a chance.

Strong bonds, loyalty,
To you I pledge my fealty.
Shadows play, I must not say,
In case you go away.
Red light, shining bright,
Make me dance with delight.
Stay strong, don't go wrong,
Keep me safe inside of you.

I Know Not

I know not where I'm going,
Or what I need to do,
I only know I have to for
My life is planned beyond,
I do not know the reasons,
I care not what it means,
I only know I have to
To see my plan fulfilled.

My mission isn't finished,
It won't be for some time,
But when it is I leave you
And go beyond the time,
Happy that I've finished,
And laboured not in vain,
I'll rest again in Heaven,
Until my next sojourn.

The Pawn

I am a pawn,
I make a move,
I hold my breath,
I live my life,
Then wait for death,
I look around,
See Kings and Queens,
But more and more
I see but pawns,
Living life, just like me.

Don't Be Sad

Let not the heart be saddened,
By things beyond our scope,
But give your God some praise,
And He will give you hope,
Let not the mind be quickened,
By things beyond our means,
But give your God some praise,
And He will give you things,
Then worship Him a little more,
And He will give you peace,
Let all your troubles fall away,
And think not of despair.

Let There Be Light

I am a light for darkened souls,
Who cannot see their path,
A beacon in the distance
To walk towards for help,
We all can be a light you know,
If only we would try,
To serve our fellow human beings
Instead of feeding greed.
If we could look beyond ourselves
And see the needs of more,
Then we could truly help the world
Defeat the grimy wars.

The Puppet

I am a puppet on a string,
With someone else in charge,
I see myself reacting,
A hundred different ways,
Sometimes I nearly pull my own,
And guide myself along,
But then I need a hand
And back I go controlled.
It's funny how these forces,
Come into play somehow,
And put me back upon my feet,
To gently let me flow,
I do not mind my strings being pulled,
I know it is for my good,
I know who is doing the pulling,
But I will never say.

Lincoln Rock

The rock looks over a vista so vast that my eyes
cannot take it all in
The hue of the eucalyptus trees a beautiful blue,
The air is fresh and crisp, like an unspoiled apple,
My heart leaps at the beauty of it all and,
In comparison I feel small.

My friend looks at the view for the first time,
She is mesmerized also,
by the magnificence before her,
Together we stand in silence,
Meditating on the quiet still splendour,
We look at each other knowing what the other is
experiencing.

In awe we make ready to leave and look once more
The distance of the trees all around us and,
No words necessary to express the joint communion,
Of nature in its purest most delightful form.

The Fountain

I sat beside the fountain eating my gelato,
The sun shining gloriously and dancing on the water,
From above a voice sang melodiously in contralto
Serenading all who had the time to hear.

I threw the coins over my shoulder,
To lay in the fountain and bring me love,
I remember with fondness now that I am older,
That the love was with me all along.

Teeth

Teeth, they hurt when we get them breaking through
the gums,
Then they fall out and more come causing more pain,
If only they were indestructible, and we could eat
what we want,
Whether vegetables, sweets, or juicy ripe plums.

Visits to the dentist are nerve wracking at best,
Not to mention the cost of consultation,
plus, all the rest,
If only we were born with all our teeth in place
Or have gums like vices with no need of teeth at all.

The Middle of the Night

I wake, it is the middle of the night,
Dark and soundless
Just how I like it to gather my thoughts,
On how I want life to be
It is my time, mine alone, no one else in sight,
Hopes and wishes boundless,
Just for me.

It isn't that I don't think of others,
But that is for another time,
When days are long and crowded
Sometimes I may feel smothered,
Much like other mothers
Then all the wants and needs are shrouded
In the middle of the night.

War

My eyes are filled with tears,
My heart is aching for the people,
Why do we hurt each other in this way,
For want of power.

Men sent to battle,
Women left back home,
Children scared and confused,
Why do we hurt each other in this way,
For want of power.

When the battle is done
Men lay dead, and women and children are alone,
What has been achieved, more land more ego,
Why do we hurt each other in this way,
For want of power.

Old Times

I saw you today, you were looking in a shop window,
I wondered if I should say hello,
Or simply go.

Too long has past for us to revisit times gone by,
Though tempting to stay and catch your eye,
Silently I say goodbye.

I'll move on and won't look back it is better this way.
Why scratch old wounds of our history?
Let them remain a mystery.

Relationships aren't easy and, some fall by the
wayside,
Ours was not meant to last forever,
No matter how much we endeavour

To make them so.

The Book

I started to write a book today,
Not knowing what it's about,
The words came flooding into my mind,
They just had to come on out.

I love the door of inspiration,
Opening to greater things
And I love to sit in wonder,
At the beauty that it brings

Through words.

A Winters Night

Take off your hat and your coat,
warm your hands and feet by the fire,
hot chocolate and all things nice
let go of the cold and the ice.
Tomorrow will come soon enough,
for now, let go of the stuff,
as your body thaws from the cold
and your mind settles down from the day,
the winter seems further away.
For the moment just rest in the warmth
the world affairs are outside,
in the coziness sit and hide.
Dream of summer and being outside
in your shorts and getting a tan
enjoying every minute that you can
Before winter is upon you again.

The Sadness

Deep down the sadness, all pervading,
it should be such a happy time,
yet I am overcome with feelings,
that threaten to swallow me whole,
from the inside out.

I don't know what it is that saddens me so,
I only know that my body is heavy with grief,
for what was or could have been,
or maybe for what never was,
I guess I will never know.

The sadness frightens me,
overwhelming other emotions
that can lift me up,
I sit in silence and feel the heaviness,
And hope that it will pass.

The Night

The night draws in, I ready myself for sleep,
The days thoughts are swirling like a cyclone,
Coming from the deep.
I breathe slow and strong, hoping for reprieve,
From the never-ending cycle of rehashed memories,
None of which I want to keep.

My breathing becomes slower and more purposeful,
Filling my lungs with precious air
As my body settles down
My mind starts unwinding the coiled mess,
Of unwanted recollections
My face lets go of the frown,

And I slip into blissful sleep.

About Connie Howell

Connie Howell is the author of several books and is a poet who lives in the Blue Mountains, West of Sydney, Australia. Her book, *Perfectly Imperfect, how to be imperfect and remain lovable*, published by Deep Read Press, was nominated for the 2022 Writers' Lounge Bookshelf Award.

Soul Deep, her first book of verse, reflects her love of expressing the depths of herself through the written word.

British by birth she migrated to Australia in 1973 and it is here that she became an author. However, in her youth while at senior school she began writing poetry but never kept a record of any of her poems.

You can find Connie on social media and on her website www.conniehowell.com.au

www.ingramcontent.com/pod-product-compliance
Lightning Source LLC
Chambersburg PA
CBHW060052050426

42448CB00011B/2419

* 9 7 8 1 9 5 4 9 8 9 2 7 6 *